Chapter 1

Who is Jezebel?

Jezebel was the princess of Tyre and Sidon and the daughter of Ethbaal, king of Tyre. She was a princess over the Sidonians.

> *And it came to pass, as though it had been a trivial thing for him to walk in the sins of Jeroboam the son of Nebat, that he took as wife Jezebel the daughter of Ethbaal, king of the Sidonians; and he went and served Baal and worshiped him* (I Kings 16:31).

She was like a bacteria in the nucleus of Israel. She was a dominant figure in leadership for 30 years. She was a woman who had 30 years of power. She was truly a woman of royalty. We find her to be the daughter of a king, the wife of a king, the mother of kings, and the grandmother of a king. She typifies and is the prime example of a horrible mother and a terrible wife. She came from a lineage of deception, conspiracy, and pandemonium. If generational curses are not broken off your life, you will often be subjected to patterns, behaviors, and mannerisms of your forefathers.

Josephus Flavius tells us that the historian Menander propounds that Ethbaal was a priest who gained his position on the throne by assassinating, Pheles, his brother. It is with this same ruthlessness and thuggery that Jezebel handled her reign as queen of Israel.

This spirit is ever so present today in the Body of Christ. This spirit will cut the throat of anyone who stands in its way. It might be notoriety, a position, fame, fortune, or advancement in the church. You must be cognizant of this spirit, because it will fester in the choir, administration, and leadership. Anyone that threatens or stands up to Jezebel is dealt with in a vicious, malicious, and vindictive way.

Jezebel was devoted to the Phoenician god, Baal, and was a zealous missionary. She was a passionate worshipper of Baal and Asherah. Baal's worship was the worship of the god of rain and storms. There were several Baals.

> *So Israel was joined to Baal of Peor, and the anger of the LORD was aroused against Israel* (Numbers 25:3).

1) Baal is known as the god of agriculture. Baal was synonymous with rainstorms that brought great harvests of vegetation. This is one of the reasons why Elijah prophesied no dew or rain until he said so. This one act demonstrated that God's prophets had life and death in their mouths.

JEZEBEL'S CHURCH

Quintessential woman of greatness.

Love:
K.H.

BY
KERVIN J. SMITH

JEZEBEL'S CHURCH
Copyright © 2003 Kervin J. Smith
All Rights Reserved

Kervin J. Smith Ministries
P.O Box 119
Short Hills, NJ 07078

ISBN: 1-59352-030-1

Published by:

Christian Services Network
1975 Janich Ranch Ct.
El Cajon, CA 92019
Toll Free: 1-866-484-6184

Unless otherwise noted, Scripture quotations are from the New King James Version of the Bible.
Copyright 1979, 1980, 1982, Thomas Nelson Inc., Publishers

No part of this publication may be reproduced, stored in a retrieval system, or transmitted in any way by any means – electronic, mechanical, photocopy, recording, or otherwise, without the prior permission of the copyright holder, except as provided by USA copyright law.

Printed in the United States of America

SPECIAL THANKS

PHINIS ASHLEY
MARIJIA BAILEY
EVELYN BANKS
LISA BANKS
REVEREND LORETTA BAZEMORE
PATRICIA H. BOBO
LA ROSA BOLTON
BISHOP JAMES BRINKLEY
TRINA BRINKLEY
KRISTON & MARIUS BROWN
EUNICE BRYANT
CAROLYN BUTTS
RENE DIGGLES
ALMA DIXON
THERESA ELLIS
JAMES & DANIELL GAMBRELL
ELLA L. HILL
JACQUELINE HOLLOMAN
LAWAYNA HOLLOMAN
VELMA M. HOLLOMAN
MARIONETTE JEFFERSON
DENISE JOHNSOM
JUNOE A. JUSTICE
LYNN LOVEJOY
ANGIE MENENDEZ
BARBARA MILLER
MAXINE MORGAN
BENNY MOYLER
ZEPHYR MOYLER
LINDA MURPHY
ELIZABETH A. PAYNE
CHARLOTTE PUTTS
RONALD WILLIAMS
KAREN YANCEY

TABLE OF CONTENTS

CHAPTER 1
   WHO IS JEZEBEL? .7
CHAPTER 2
   THE CHURCH OF THYATIRA 21
CHAPTER 3
   SPIRIT OF MANIPULATION 37
CHAPTER 4
   SPIRIT OF INTIMIDATION 47

And Elijah the Tishbite, of the inhabitants of Gilead, said to Ahab, "As the LORD God of Israel lives, before whom I stand, there shall not be dew nor rain these years, except at my word" (I Kings 17:1).

The fall and spring rains were necessary for the vegetation of Israel. The Lord refused to allow their crops to continue to grow as long as they served other gods.

> *Take heed to yourselves, lest your heart be deceived, and you turn aside and serve other gods and worship them, lest the LORD'S anger be aroused against you, and He shut up the heavens so that there be no rain, and the land yield no produce, and you perish quickly from the good land which the LORD is giving you* (Deuteronomy 11:16-17).

Elijah spoke the drought into existence and God answered his word. This showed that Baal was not sufficient before the Lord.

The name Baal means "lord, husband, owner." It is also believed that Baal was the son of Dagon. He is given the names "the Prince," "the Powerful," and "the rider of clouds." There are several other Baals that are mentioned in the scriptures.

2) The Baal of Peor talked about sexual immorality with the women of Moab. Moab was identified with sexual immorality, and incestuous relationships. Moab was the son that was conceived by Lot's daughter after she and her father engaged in a sexual affair. The name Moab means "my fatherless seed."

> *Then Lot went up out of Zoar and dwelt in the mountains, and his two daughters were*

with him; for he was afraid to dwell in Zoar. And he and his two daughters dwelt in a cave.

Now the firstborn said to the younger, Our father is old, and there is no man on the earth to come in to us as is the custom of all the earth.

Come, let us make our father drink wine, and we will lie with him, that we may preserve the lineage of our father.

So they made their father drink wine that night. And the firstborn went in and lay with her father, and he did not know when she lay down or when she arose.

It happened on the next day that the firstborn said to the younger, Indeed I lay with my father last night; let us make him drink wine tonight also, and you go in and lie with him, that we may preserve the lineage of our father.

Then they made their father drink wine that night also. And the younger arose and lay with him, and he did not know when she lay down or when she arose.

Thus both the daughters of Lot were with child by their father.

The firstborn bore a son and called his name Moab; he is the father of the Moabites to this day (Genesis 19:30-37).

The Moabites were part of a pagan cult. The Israelites participated in these sexually immoral acts. The Israelites then found themselves connected to this god Baal of Peor.

And it was so, as soon as Gideon was dead,

*that the children of Israel again played the harlot with the Baals, and made **Baal-Berith** their god* (Judges 8:33).

*So they gave him seventy shekels of silver from the temple of **Baal-Berith**, with which Abimelech hired worthless and reckless men; and they followed him* (Judges 9:4).

*Now Ahaziah fell through the lattice of his upper room in Samaria, and was injured; so he sent messengers and said to them, Go inquire of **Baal-Zebub**, the god of Ekron, whether I shall recover from this injury.*

But the angel of the LORD said to Elijah the Tishbite, Arise, go up to meet the messengers of the king of Samaria, and say to them, 'Is it because there is no God in Israel that you are going to inquire of Baal-Zebub, the god of Ekron? (II Kings 1:2-3)

Solomon had a vineyard at Baal Hamon (Song of Solomon 8:11a).

So Ahab sent for all the children of Israel, and gathered the prophets together on Mount Carmel.

This is one of the classic texts in the Old Testament. It speaks of the confrontation between God's prophet, Elijah, and Jezebel's prophets. This text speaks of good versus evil, and light versus darkness. One true prophet versus 850 false prophets.

And Elijah came to all the people, and said, How long will you falter between two opinions? If the LORD is God, follow Him; but if Baal, then follow him. But the people answered him not a word.

Then Elijah said to the people, I alone am left a prophet of the LORD; but Baal's prophets are four hundred and fifty men.

Therefore let them give us two bulls; and let them choose one bull for themselves, cut it in pieces, and lay it on the wood, but put no fire under it; and I will prepare the other bull, and lay it on the wood, but put no fire under it.

Then you call on the name of your gods, and I will call on the name of the LORD; and the God who answers by fire, He is God. So all the people answered and said, It is well spoken.

Now Elijah said to the prophets of Baal, Choose one bull for yourselves and prepare it first, for you are many; and call on the name of your god, but put no fire under it.

So they took the bull which was given them, and they prepared it, and called on the name of Baal from morning even till noon, saying, O Baal, hear us! But there was no voice; no one answered. And they leaped about the altar which they had made.

And so it was, at noon, that Elijah mocked them and said, Cry aloud, for he is a god; either he is meditating, or he is busy, or he is on a journey, or perhaps he is sleeping and must be awakened.

So they cried aloud, and cut themselves, as was their custom, with knives and lances, until the blood gushed out on them.

And it was so, when midday was past, that they prophesied until the time of the offering of the evening sacrifice. But there was no voice; no one answered, no one paid attention.

Then Elijah said to all the people, Come near to me. So all the people came near to him. And he repaired the altar of the LORD that was broken down.

And Elijah took twelve stones, according to the number of the tribes of the sons of Jacob, to whom the word of the LORD had come, saying, Israel shall be your name.

Then with the stones he built an altar in the name of the LORD; and he made a trench around the altar large enough to hold two seahs of seed.

And he put the wood in order, cut the bull in pieces, and laid it on the wood, and said, Fill four waterpots with water, and pour it on the burnt sacrifice and on the wood.

Then he said, Do it a second time, and they did it a second time; and he said, Do it a third time, and they did it a third time.

So the water ran all around the altar; and he also filled the trench with water.

And it came to pass, at the time of the offering of the evening sacrifice, that Elijah the prophet came near and said, LORD God of Abraham, Isaac, and Israel, let it be known this day that You are God in Israel, and that I am Your servant, and that I have done all these things at Your word.

Hear me, O LORD, hear me, that this people may know that You are the LORD God, and that You have turned their hearts back to You again.

Then the fire of the LORD fell and consumed the burnt sacrifice, and the wood and the stones and the dust, and it licked water that was in the trench.

Now when all the people saw it, they fell on their faces; and they said, The LORD, He is God! The LORD, He is God!

And Elijah said to them, Seize the prophets of Baal! Do not let one of them escape! So they seized them; and Elijah brought them down to the Brook Kishon and executed them there (I Kings 18:20-40).

Then the word of the LORD came to Elijah the Tishbite, saying,

Arise, go down to meet Ahab king of Israel, who lives in Samaria. There he is, in the vineyard of Naboth, where he has gone down to take possession of it.

You shall speak to him, saying, Thus says the LORD: Have you murdered and also taken possession?" And you shall speak to him, saying, Thus says the LORD: In the place where dogs licked the blood of Naboth, dogs shall lick your blood, even yours.

Then Ahab said to Elijah, Have you found me, O my enemy? And he answered, I have found you, because you have sold yourself to do evil in the sight of the LORD.

Behold, I will bring calamity on you. I will take away your posterity, and will cut off from Ahab every male in Israel, both bond and free.

I will make your house like the house of Jeroboam the son of Nebat, and like the house of Baasha the son of Ahijah, because of the provocation with which you have provoked Me to anger, and made Israel sin.

And concerning Jezebel the LORD also spoke, saying, The dogs shall eat Jezebel by the wall of Jezreel.

The dogs shall eat whoever belongs to Ahab and dies in the city, and the birds of the air shall eat whoever dies in the field.

But there was no one like Ahab who sold himself to do wickedness in the sight of the LORD, because Jezebel his wife stirred him up.

And he behaved very abominably in following idols, according to all that the Amorites had done, whom the LORD had cast out before the children of Israel.

So it was, when Ahab heard those words, that he tore his clothes and put sackcloth on his body, and fasted and lay in sackcloth, and went about mourning.

And the word of the LORD came to Elijah the Tishbite, saying,

See how Ahab has humbled himself before Me? Because he has humbled himself before Me, I will not bring the calamity in his days; but in the days of his son I will bring the calamity on his house" (I Kings 21:17-29).

God sent Elijah to pronounce judgment upon him. Ahab had a repentant heart, and because of that God delayed his punishment.

God also gave grace to Jezebel's punishment. God gave her time to repent. However, instead of repenting she coerced her sons to do the same sins.

The reign of Jezebel from Thyatira not repenting informs us that she was committed to spiritual and intellectual suicide. People who have a relationship with God are seeking God for themselves. Most of the people that follow Jezebel are insecure and co-dependent.

This deep doctrine she had catered to was self-will. She made fornication, adultery, and love on the same plane. She encouraged the people to eat food sacrificed to other gods and commit lewd sexual activities. She followed the pattern of the Nicolaitans. She, like the Nicolaitans, led believers into idolatry and immorality.

Jezebel had a constituency of 850 prophets who were at her beck and call. She had an entourage of eunuchs who engaged in orgies and lewd sexual activity. She is called the Lady Macbeth of the Old Testament. She is likened to Mary, Queen of Scots. Scholars have also compared her to Marie Antoinette and Catherine de Medici. Jezebel represents the apex of what a dreadful woman can be.

Jezebel was such a controlling woman that she controlled her husband and ran the nation. Ahab was merely a figurehead. Her first order of business was to abolish the prophets of the Lord.

For so it was, while Jezebel massacred the prophets of the LORD, that Obadiah had taken one hundred prophets and hidden them, fifty to a cave, and had fed them with bread and water (I Kings 18:4).

Her arch nemesis was the prophet Elijah, who fought her to the end. Elijah demanded a contest on Mount Carmel between the powers of Israel's God and the powers of Jezebel's god, Baal. The test was whether the prophets of Baal could bring rain after the long drought; they did not accomplish their mission. Elijah prayed, and God answered his prayers. Jezebel was so upset with Elijah that she put out a contract on the life of the prophet. Elijah prophesied that every member of the house of Ahab and Jezebel would be dishonored in death.

And concerning Jezebel the LORD also spoke, saying, 'The dogs shall eat Jezebel by the wall of Jezreel (I Kings 21:23).

Jezebel outlived her husband by ten years. Even after Ahab died, she still was very controlling. She was still the force over Israel and controlled Israel through her eldest son Ahaziah, who was a worshipper of Baal. After being king for two years he fell from a window and died.

Jezebel's youngest son, Jehoram, ruled for seven years. During his reign, Jehu was delegated by Elijah to overthrow the Ahab dynasty; Jehu came to Jehoram and announced there would be no peace in Israel.

Now it happened, when Jehoram saw Jehu, that he said, Is it peace, Jehu? So he answered, What peace, as long as the harlotries of your mother Jezebel and her witchcraft are so many? (II Kings 9:22)

Jehoram was also murdered by Jehu. It was Jezebel who faced the most heinous death of all. She knew that her end was near; the kings of Israel and Judah had already suffered death. Yet she continued to adorn herself. She adorned herself with makeup made of a black powder mixed with oil and applied to make her appear distinctive.

And when Jehu had come to Jezreel, Jezebel heard of it; and she put paint on her eyes and adorned her head, and looked through a window.

Then, as Jehu entered at the gate, she said, Is it peace, Zimri, murderer of your master?

And he looked up at the window, and said, Who is on my side? Who? And two or three eunuchs looked out at him.

Then he said, Throw her down. So they threw her down, and some of her blood spattered on the wall and on the horses; and he trampled her under foot.

And when he had gone in, he ate and drank. Then he said, Go now, see to this accursed woman, and bury her, for she was a king's daughter.

So they went to bury her, but they found no more of her than the skull and the feet and the palms of her hands.

Therefore they came back and told him. And he said, This is the word of the LORD, which He spoke by His servant Elijah the Tishbite, saying, 'On the plot of ground at Jezreel dogs shall eat the flesh of Jezebel;

And the corpse of Jezebel shall be as refuse on the surface of the field, in the plot at Jezreel, so that they shall not say, "Here lies Jezebel" ' " (II Kings 9:30-37).

CHAPTER 2

THE CHURCH OF THYATIRA

And to the angel of the church in Thyatira write, These things says the Son of God, who has eyes like a flame of fire, and His feet like fine brass:

I know your works, love, service, faith, and your patience; and as for your works, the last are more than the first.

Nevertheless I have a few things against you, because you allow that woman Jezebel, who calls herself a prophetess, to teach and seduce My servants to commit sexual immorality and eat things sacrificed to idols.

And I gave her time to repent of her sexual immorality, and she did not repent.

> *Indeed I will cast her into a sickbed, and those who commit adultery with her into great tribulation, unless they repent of their deeds.*
>
> *I will kill her children with death, and all the churches shall know that I am He who searches the minds and hearts. And I will give to each one of you according to your works.*
>
> *Now to you I say, and to the rest in Thyatira, as many as do not have this doctrine, who have not known the depths of Satan, as they say, I will put on you no other burden*
>
> *But hold fast what you have till I come.*
>
> *And he who overcomes, and keeps My works until the end, to him I will give power over the nations (Revelation 2:18-26).*

The letter to the church in Thyatira covers the central period in the church's history. It was again a period of persecution. It covered what we speak of as the Dark Ages, in which a harlot had usurped power in the church of Jesus Christ. There was a spirit of pandemonium, and people did what was right in their own eyes.

In this letter to the church at Thyatira, Jesus introduces himself by a phrase that is not used anywhere else in Revelation. He uses the name "Son of God." The Son of God describes Jesus' relationship to God. He discusses divine sonship. This title could very well be called the most Christological title in the New Testament.

> *But these are written that you may believe that Jesus is the Christ, the Son of God, and that believing you may have life in His name (John 20:31).*
>
> *And we know that the Son of God has come and has given us an understanding, that we*

may know Him who is true; and we are in Him who is true, in His Son Jesus Christ. This is the true God and eternal life (I John 5:20).

How was the church established at Thyatira? We really do not know who started the church. Here is what we do know about Thyatira. It was approximately thirty to forty miles southeast of Pergamos, the central important center of the wool trade. A guild of wool workers was based there. The only person with whom the Bible acquaints us with that has ever lived in this city is a woman named Lydia. Thyatira was known for its great commercial prosperity and wealth.

After Paul went to Philippi he was on the outskirts of the city. Paul made a trip there, and sat down and ministered to a group of women. It was not a formal meeting, but Paul made an impact on lives everywhere he went. He made a tremendous impression on these women. There was a woman there who had been affected greatly. The Bible tells us her name was Lydia.

She was touched by God and received Paul's message. She was a brilliant woman who was converted, and a seller of purple from Thyatira.

And from there he went to Philippi, which is the foremost city of that part of Macedonia, a colony. And we were staying in that city for some days.

And on the Sabbath day we went out of the city to the river side, where prayer was customarily made; and we sat down and spoke to the women who met there.

Now a certain woman named Lydia heard us. She was a seller of purple from the city of

Thyatira, who worshiped God. The Lord opened her heart to heed the things spoken by Paul.

And when she and her household were baptized, she begged us, saying, If you have judged me to be faithful to the Lord, come to my house and stay. And she constrained us (Acts 16:12-15).

Lydia was a businesswoman, a "seller of purple," and probably was one of the wealthiest women in Philippi. Lydia was a woman of insight, foresight, and determination. She probably wore purple well, and dressed in her fashions as she walked the streets of Philippi selling her purple. Thyatira was near a chief river, and it was believed the water was well-adapted for dying. The purple dye in this city could not be produced anywhere else. Thyatira was universally known for its ability to produce the perfect purple dye. Purple dye came from two sources: (a) madder root which grew plentifully around Thyatira; (b) shellfish, which contained the best dye.

John lays the foundation about the beauty of the church, then he gives us the six commendations from Jesus.

I know your works, love, service, faith, and your patience; and as for your works, the last are more than the first (Revelation 2:19).

I know your works" (Revelation 2:19)

The first commendation he gives is "I know thy works." Their <u>charity</u>. They have ministered to the poor and distressed.

"I know thy love" (Revelation 2:19)

The second commendation is "I know thy love." Thyatira had kept the love of Christ at the epicenter of the church. The church still had a passion for the things of God. They decided to love God with an irreverent passion. I know that you have kept me in your hearts. I know that you have an undying love for me and you love your brothers also.

I know you have a passion for me. I am indelibly etched on your hearts. You are passionately dedicated to me, loving me, and you love your brother. This is one of the most powerful things that Jesus can say about us. If Jesus can speak that about you in spite of your idiosyncrasies, you have the mark of a Christian.

By this shall men know that ye are my disciples, if ye have love one to another.

"I know thy service" (Revelation 2:19)

The third commendation is "I know thy service." In today's society, you have taken care of widows, orphans, unwed mothers, homeless, and substance abusers.

"I know thy faith" (Revelation 2:19)

The fourth commendation is "Thy faith." Faith is a treasure, it is the key to the entrance way to commune with God. There is no pleasing God without it.

But without faith it is impossible to please Him, for he who comes to God must believe that He is, and that He is a rewarder of those who diligently seek Him (Hebrews 11:6).

"I know thy patience" (Revelation 2:19)

The fifth commendation is "Thy patience." Patience means the power to wait, and the power to endure. Jesus was the master at waiting. To be patient is to be like Jesus. The church at Thyatira possessed patience. Jesus was saying you have persevered under afflictions and persecutions.

"I know thy works" (Revelation 2:19)

The sixth commendation was "Thy works." Your continued labors of love and obedience. "The last to be more than the first."

You not only kept what you retained, but you grew in grace, and in the knowledge and love of Jesus.

Most churches have lost their power and their worship. Most churches require a spiritual cardiopulmonary resuscitation (C.P.R.). A revival is what is needed to bring the church back to life. Not driven by personality-oriented Christians, but people who are yielded to the things of God. God is not looking for golden vessels, silver vessels, or bronze vessels. He is just looking for a yielded vessel.

One of the clear reasons that we need spiritual C.P.R. is that we have lost our pulse. Is it possible that the church is not breathing, and we need life support? The church is supposed to be a hospital. We should receive the lost, the sick, the homosexual, the lesbian, the demon-possessed, the adulterer, the fornicator, the drug addicted, the entertainer, the politician and any soul that needs life.

We cannot become an effective hospital, because we are in the intensive care unit ourselves. When a restaurant is deemed unsatisfactory by the inspectors, they are given a grade according to their establishment. Is the place clean? Is the kitchen area in order? How is the food prepared?

Is it sanitary in the front of the restaurant as well as the back? They are given grades from A through F. Of course A is the best; to go into a B-graded restaurant is unsatisfactory. You expect the top grade when you eat at a restaurant. You are not worried about what you see; it's what you do not see that disturbs you. After several visits from the inspector, if they have not conformed to the codes they will shut them down. What do you do when the church has not conformed to the code of the most thorough Inspector? We are in a day and hour where God is going to start shutting down people who are not conforming to code. There have to be some Christians who are seeking to conform to Godly codes. What grade do you deserve? Are you an A, B, C, D, or F Christian? What codes are you conforming to? God is calling us to maximize ourselves within Him.

*And to the angel of the church in Thyatira write, These things says the Son of God, who has eyes like a **flame of fire**, and His **feet like fine brass*** (Revelation 2:18).

His eyes are as a **flame of fire**; that is, his eyes are like spiritual laser beams that see the heart and the depth of things. He reads you, and He reads the position of the church. His eyes not only see you where you are, but see where you are going. His eyes look into the idiosyncrasies of the church. This is why he is called omnipresent. He is the God that is on His way to where He just came from; and will pass Himself in the process.

His feet are like fine brass (Revelation 2:18b)

Brass feet are a clear reference to divine judgment. With His feet, He treads down all the powers of the devil. Christ's feet are like brass burning in the furnace. The first part of Jesus ever mentioned in the scripture is His feet.

He shall bruise your head, and you shall bruise His heel (Genesis 3:15).

If you do an in-depth study on the feet of the Lord Jesus Christ, you will see that His... feet were washed with the woman's tears and wiped with the hairs of her head; the first part of the Lord's body which was touched after He rose from the dead was His feet; the woman clasped His feet and the feet of Jesus were bruised by the serpent.

Nevertheless I have a few things against you, because you allow that <u>woman Jezebel</u>, who calls herself a prophetess, to teach and beguile My servants to commit sexual immorality and to eat things sacrificed to idols (Revelation 2:20).

"**That woman Jezebel**" was a woman of power and influence in Thyatira who brought about the spirit of corruption.

This spirit was deliberately leading the people away from the things of God. She had the same spirit as Jezebel in the Old Testament.

The first Jezebel was dead nearly a thousand years.

There is an allusion here to the history of Ahab and Jezebel. We do not know who this Jezebel was: she was a woman who had power and influence. She tainted and corrupted the true religion and harassed the followers of God in that city, as Jezebel did in Israel.

The evil spirit of Jezebel had been incarnated in a prophetess. She encouraged the Christians of Thyatira to participate in ceremonies and feasts of a pagan deity. She taught the Christians that fornication, and eating things offered to idols, were matters of indifference, and thus they were seduced from the truth. She was not a real prophetess, but a false prophetess, who was very shrewd.

Nevertheless I have a few things against you, because you allow that woman Jezebel, who calls herself a prophetess, to teach and seduce My servants to commit sexual immorality and eat things sacrificed to idols (Revelation 2:20).

"**Thy wife Jezebel**" was the wife of the bishop of the church, and the indictment was against him as well because he did not set things in order. He was walking in the spirit of Ahab. Jezebel is not effective unless she has an Ahab. Ahab represents weak leadership. He is a leader who has no control over his church, business, home, or situation.

That woman Jezebel, who calls herself a prophetess (Revelation 2:20b).

"**She called herself a prophetess**." She was a possessor and preacher of a false faith. The fact that she was a prophetess gave her a position of authority.

What did this prophetess teach? She propagated heresy in the church of Thyatira. She called it "the deep things." This woman set herself up as a teacher.

The bishop had the ability to shut her down, as well as remove her party from the church. He could have placed a restraint on his wife, but he did not do it, he gave her every opportunity to seduce the faithful. You listen, and you tolerate this woman who calls herself a prophetess. She is making false claims as being God's spokesman. We have no idea who she really was. Certainly her real name is not Jezebel.

The name was given to indicate the kind of woman she was, and the influence she had on people who came in contact with her. Jezebel was faithful to a false faith. She was a woman highly placed. She represents royalty.

The word *prophetis*; genitive *prophetidos*, feminine noun from *prophemi* - means to tell beforehand, or to forthtell. Which is *pro* - before or forth, and *phemi* - to tell. By calling herself a prophetess she was actually saying that she spoke on behalf of God. There are three things every prophet or prophetess possesses. They possess sight, insight, or foresight.

With sight they see, with insight they inspect, with foresight they speak forth. She called herself a prophetess, she was a possessor and preacher of a false faith. The fact that she was a prophetess gave her a position of authority. What did this prophetess teach? She propagated heresy in the church of Thyatira. She called it "the deep things." This woman set herself up as the teacher. She taught the saints that fornication and eating things offered to idols were okay. The scholars tell us this fornication meant to serve other gods.

The bishop had the power to shut Jezebel down, but he did not. He chose to allow her to spread theological bacteria throughout this church. If pastors do not deal with Jezebel, they will experience rebellion, witchcraft and division.

This woman taught the Christians that fornication and eating things offered to idols were matters of indifference, and thus they were seduced from the truth.

She was not a real prophetess, but a false prophetess, who was very shrewd. She correlated the sexual immorality of the Nicolaitans and brought their heresy into the church.

This prophetess was a promulgator of a false faith.

Because she was a prophetess, it gave her a place of honor. Because she was the pastor's wife, that would validate her position. This woman had the ability to hoodwink, bamboozle, become your friend, and influence you at the same time. Those who walk in the spirit of Jezebel are master communicators, have tremendous influence, high ranking positions, and are master manipulators. Jezebel can only be effective if she has some sort of rank or position. This is what validates her, and makes her influence so powerful.

Jezebel, who calls herself a prophetess, to teach and seduce My servants to commit sexual immorality and eat things sacrificed to idols (Revelation 2:20c).

"**The deep things**" What did Jezebel teach? We do not have a clue what she propagated. But what we do know, was that she called it "the deep things." A person that is shallow concerning the things of God, or has an insatiable appetite for something different, will subscribe to this type of evil. In other words, Jezebel was married to her sin. To lose the quest to walk in the blessings of God, and have no desire to repent, you have already begun to die.

Then immediately an angel of the Lord struck him, because he did not give glory to God. And he was eaten by worms and died (Acts 12:23).

According to the Gnostic school of thought, "since matter was evil the sins of the flesh could be indulged without damage to the spirit." The Jezebelites had the same belief as the Nicolatians and the Balaamites. She correlated the sexual immorality of the Nicolatians and brought their heresy over to the church. They also were people who practiced immorality and the eating of food sacrificed to idols.

The church was allowing Jezebel to go unchecked. The church of Thyatira was very weak and spineless toward the new Jezebel. It was her goal to place the Christians at Thyatira in spiritual bondage.

"I know" Jesus acts as a Heavenly Manager. *The church itself does not know what is going on behind closed doors, but Jesus knows* (Revelation 2:19).

You tolerated this woman Jezebel, who calls herself a prophetess, and her teaching leads my servants astray, so that they commit fornication. She has placed a spiritual anesthetic on your mind, and destroyed your sensitivity to sin. This opened the door to moral and spiritual destruction.

The church itself does not know what is going on behind closed doors, but Jesus knows.

And I gave her time to repent of her sexual immorality, and she did not repent (Revelation 2:21).

I gave her time to repent: She refused to repent of her immorality.

If Jezebel would not repent, there is still a glimmer of hope for her followers: Those who commit adultery with her will surely be punished, unless they repent of their doings.

The door of repentance was still open. There was still time. But the door would not be open long. One day it would be shut.

But to you I say, and to the rest in Thyatira, as many as do not have this doctrine, and who have not known the depths of Satan, as they call them,

I will put on you no other burden (Revelation 2:24).

There was still a godly remnant in Thyatira who had not defiled themselves. These are people who refused to subscribe to "the deep things" of Jezebel.

Christ urges them to hold fast to what they have. Winds may come and go, but we must lay hold to the foundation God has planted us in.

Hold fast to what we already have, that is to say, what he has already given us in His written word. Let us hold fast to the things of God. We must live according to scripture.

Therefore let that abide in you which you heard from the beginning. If what you heard from the beginning abides in you, you also will abide in the Son and in the Father (I John 2:24).

Therefore, brethren, stand fast and hold the traditions which you were taught, whether by word or our epistle (II Thessalonians 2:15).

Now these things, brethren, I have figuratively transferred to myself and Apollos for your sakes, that you may learn in us not to think beyond what is written, that none of you may be puffed up on behalf of one against the other (I Corinthians 4:6).

Be sure to hold on to the foundations of holiness. Anything that is contrary to God's word is error. If someone is trying to introduce you to "deep things," and the Bible is not the center, remove yourself from those people, or the situation. There are many religious and teachings out there. To name a few of those religions teachings available. The New Age Movement,

Buddhism, The Mar-Movement, the doctrine of inclusion, and many more religions. Keep yourself focused on the things of God, not the "deep things."

Jesus is calling the church to repentance. There are people today who have the same spirit. They are engaged in all manners of sin, and refuse to have a repentant heart.

They have become so engulfed in their beliefs and their sins that they actually believe they are right. We have deacons, ushers, choir members, and leaders who are walking with this type of spirit in the church. One of the greatest problems in Christendom today is that there is no desire to repent. I have had the pleasure of speaking in some of the greatest churches in America. As I travel around the world, I do not see a sense of repentance.

One of the reasons there is no repentance is because there is no reverence. There is no real reason to repent before God. We have prosperity conferences, healing crusades, family conferences, etc.... When is the last time you went to a soul-winners' conference? I respect every one of these conferences, but we have to get back to the basics. Somewhere we got off track, and we have looked at souls as the last part of the service. People tend to want to use God like He is a spiritual genie. Thank you Lord for my car, my home, my job. But after we obtain the blessings of God, we place Him on a shelf until Sunday morning. Whenever there is a need we repent. If someone is losing their home, if you desire God to save your mate, if you need God to bring you out of a financial dilemma, and if you need God to heal you or a loved one, these are the times we need to repent.

And I will give him the morning star (Revelation 2:28).

"**I will give him the morning star**" The "morning star" is Jesus. "I am the bright and morning star." This name is very significant. The times were perilous, and very dark. It looked very dim for the church at Thyatira. Just as today we are facing a crucial time in our nation. Times are the darkest in our history. We are in an unprecedented time of darkness. Our nation is under attack. The United States is at war in Afghanistan, and in Iraq. The times are very bleak, terrorist activities have become commonplace. Our nation is in upheaval, and the church is in a lethargic and apathetic state. We need to receive Jesus now, more than ever. The word darkness in Hebrew is the word *skotizo* - which means to deprive of light. Jesus is offering hope for a better tomorrow for the Christians of Thyatira, as He is for us. Once you receive the Light, we have to share that light with others. Jesus is the hope for a world that is in despair. He is the Light of the world.

Chapter 3

Spirit of Manipulation

One of Jezebel's most effective tools is verbal abuse. This is one of her major components of control. Control is the vehicle that she uses to run her church, her business, and her family. Every opportunity she gets to belittle you she does. She does not like the way you talk, your hair, your clothes, your makeup, the way you worship, and even the car you drive. The dress you wore to church is too tight, too short, does not look right on you, is not your color, you look like an absolute idiot in that outfit. The car you drive is too expensive for you. Your makeup looks cheap, or you are wearing too much. What she is really saying is that she is mad that she cannot be you. The abuse is always shocking and incomprehensible. The more controlling and abusive she is, the more power she has over you. In her heart she has to do everything she can possibly do to diminish you, her goal is to feel superior to you. We oftentimes hear about bosses abusing employees, husbands abusing wives, wives abusing husbands, children abusing parents, and parents abusing children.

There is another abuse; it is called spiritual abuse. This is when someone who has been given God-authorized authority and uses that authority to abuse God's people. You become a spiritual warlock, and control God's people for your own self-aggrandizement.

Controlling behaviors are implemented through verbal abuse. Whether control is exercised verbally or physically, the dynamics are the same. The abuser controls not only your perceptions, but your self-awareness. The verbal abuser refuses to accept any responsibility for their behavior. In other words, they avoid accountability by blaming others and this allows them to stay in control.

When someone who is abusive criticizes and berates you the feelings of powerlessness are dispelled by the display of superiority.

Criticism, for example, is a display of superiority - a display of superior knowledge. Jezebel wants to believe that she knows better than the one she is criticizing, and is therefore more superior or more powerful.

Jezebel feels confident about controlling another person when she can in some way have authority over that person as a judge has over a defendant.

It is the same kind of control a policeman has over a driver, and a dictator has over his country by limiting freedom of action and freedom of dissent.

This is one of the reasons she is so verbally abusive.

Anyone who verbally abuses another, does so to maintain some form of control over the other, and to keep their own feelings of powerlessness under control. Jezebel wants you to feel powerless. It is her goal to break you down to your lowest point. The more she breaks you down, the more control she has over you.

This is one of the reasons she had so much power over Ahab.

But Jezebel his wife came to him, and said to him, Why is your spirit so sullen that you eat no food?

He said to her, Because I spoke to Naboth the Jezreelite, and said to him, Give me your vineyard for money; or else, if it pleases you, I will give you another vineyard for it: And he answered, I will not give you my vineyard.

Then Jezebel his wife said to him, You now exercise authority over Israel! Arise, and eat food, and let your heart be cheerful; I will give you the vineyard of Naboth the Jezreelite.

So she wrote letters in Ahab's name, sealed them with his seal, and sent the letters to the elders and the nobles who were dwelling in the city with Naboth.

And she wrote in the letters, saying, Proclaim a fast, and seat Naboth with high honor among the people; and seat two men, scoundrels, before him to bear witness against him, saying, You have blasphemed God and the king. Then take him out, and stone him, that he may die.

> *So the men of his city, the elders and nobles who were inhabitants of his city, did as Jezebel had sent to them, as it was written in the letters which she had sent to them.*
>
> *They proclaimed a fast, and seated Naboth with high honor among the people. And two men, scoundrels, came in and sat before him; and the scoundrels witnessed against him, against Naboth, in the presence of the people, saying, Naboth has blasphemed God and the king! Then they took him outside the city and stoned him with stones, so that he died.*
>
> *Then they sent to Jezebel, saying, Naboth has been stoned and is dead.*
>
> *And it came to pass, when Jezebel heard that Naboth had been stoned and was dead, that Jezebel said to Ahab, Arise, take possession of the vineyard of Naboth the Jezreelite, which he refused to give you for money; for Naboth is not alive, but dead.*
>
> *So it was, when Ahab heard that Naboth was dead, that Ahab got up and went down to take possession of the vineyard of Naboth the Jezreelite*
>
> (I Kings 21:7-16).

Ahab attempted to negotiate for this valuable piece of real estate. Naboth could not sell the land of his forefathers. Rather than allow the situation to die down, Jezebel intervened to get the land for her husband. This was a valuable piece of real estate that Ahab wanted for his vacation home. Jezebel superseded her husband's authority, and developed a plan to get the land anyway.

The text is very clear, how she bamboozled her husband. There was nothing he could do because Jezebel had complete control over him. As long as Jezebel has an Ahab, she will always have power. Ahab is symbolic of weak leadership or a weak man.

Jezebel wants you to feel powerless. Her primary goal is to break you down to the lowest common denominator. She actually discerns or discovers vulnerability in the individual. This spirit of control attaches itself to the weakest part of an individual.

This would be equivalent to a parent who consistently abuses a six-year-old child. You are ugly, you are stupid, you will never amount to anything. This keeps tearing away at the emotional stability of that child. It attacks the esteem a child needs. Every child needs self-worth, self-actualization, and a healthy self-esteem.

Here are a couple of examples of women who have experienced the control of a Jezebel.

Girl (22):

Someone so verbally abused she never looks up, and always has her head down. This young girl was sexually abused by her father. When her mother finds out, she tells her daughter, "It is your fault. I do not know why your father would want you. You are dumb, stupid, and ugly."

This child has been sexually abused, and mentally abused. The father is controlling her sexually, and the mother is destroying her mentally. There are a lot of people who are going through the same kind of situations. This young lady became free, and today is moving mightily in the things of God. She allowed God to break the spirit of abuse that had been over her life.

If there is anyone, or any situation that has had power over you through physical, mental and verbal abuse, it is time for you to be free.

A person that abuses you speaks death to you. Teachers can be abusive, parents can be abusive, ministers can be abusive, and spouses can be abusive. The definition of the word abuse is abnormal use.

<u>Woman (34)</u>:

Mother makes her daughter feel as if she were a mistake. She tears down the self-esteem of her daughter. I do not want you to be anything other than perfect. She tries to live her life through her daughter. Mother regretted mistakes she made, so she wants to control her daughter's life. Daughter gets straight A's and one A minus. This mother does not congratulate her daughter. She places emphasis on the A minus.

These children then develop a perfectionist attitude. She becomes the family manager, and attempts to keep things running smoothly. One of the reasons is because the parent's behavior is so inconsistent and unpredictable. They take on the duty of providing some structure and consistency for themselves and others in their family. As the oldest or only child they feel the need to be a rescuer. You see words like responsible, achieving, mature and reliable. They grow up fast, taking on adult responsibilities long before they are physically or emotionally ready.

The desire for perfection and achievement will follow the perfectionist through school, and into their adult life. Most perfectionists will have considerable success in life, but are plagued by disturbing feelings and nagging self-doubts.

There is an inward feeling that no matter what you achieve, it will never be good enough, because you believe you will never be good enough. If you have taken on a perfectionist role, you are experiencing continuous dissatisfaction and restlessness.

Though perfectionism can drive you to achieve, it may also be your greatest impediment to achievement and material success. Your attention to detail is an asset, but more of your time is spent getting others' approval than getting the job done. You may look good to others, but you do not feel good to yourself.

Because you are so intense and dedicated, it may be hard for you to keep a balance in your life. There is no middle ground for you - it is all the way or nothing at all. You will commit 110 percent to a project, or not give yourself to it at all.

People that are perfectionists tend to gravitate toward others who will support their seriousness and rigidity, rather than people who will challenge and stimulate them.

The same young lady was also told, even as an adult, everything you have is because of me. You are not the brightest one in the family, and you are here because I allowed you to be here. This young lady was so distraught and discontented, that she could not even make a decision without seeking advice from her mother. Through much prayer and fasting, she finally became free.

Jezebel does not only work through churches. She can work through a mother, an employer, or any position of authority.

Her strength comes in having "yes-people" around her. If you try to buck against her, she will retaliate against you. This woman is a backbiter, liar, and a master control freak. She is always trying to destroy the credibility of people who speak out against her.

Often leaders convey their abuse through the pulpit. Now they have a larger audience, and the more people they have under their control, the more powerful they feel.

These people will not confront individuals one on one, but will use the pulpit as a platform to convey their message. Their message brings humiliation, embarrassment, and frustration. They in essence become spiritual warlocks. They become witchcraft workers in the midst of a people who are seeking the higher things of God.

The spirit of control is used to set the precedence: if you do not conform you will face the wrath of Jezebel.

There are levels of control because you oftentimes have smaller Jezebels in a church. There will always be a Queen Jezebel who will have reign over the other Jezebels. Jezebel can only be effective if she has an Ahab to have control over. While Jezebel is operating, you have absolutely no control over your life. But you will do anything you possibly can to please Jezebel.

The belief in the need and right to control another can be instilled in a person from their early years in childhood. Jezebel learned the power of control from her childhood.

Abusers are so good at control that they can intimidate by a look, a gesture, or something as simple as a motion. Their behavior originates with the abuser needing to control their mate, as well as their own feelings of powerlessness. Jezebel does this by diminishing you, and venting her feelings toward you, while blaming you for them.

Six Categories of Verbal Abuse and Control

1) Accusing and blaming: You are to blame for your pain and whatever I say or do to you, and for everything that is not the way I want it to be.

2) Judging and criticizing: Telling you what is wrong with your thoughts and actions, I place myself over you and therefore in control of you.

3) Underminer: erode your confidence, and extinguish your determination, weaken or ruin you by degree.

4) Threatening: I am in control, do what I say.

5) Ordering and demanding: I have complete control over you. You will do as I demand.

6) Name calling: Someone is saying you do not exist. You are annihilated.

Abuse is never about conflict, it is about control. Rather than deal with their own inadequacies, the abusers feel better about themselves, when they tear other people down.

The moment you take control out of the hands of Jezebel she loses her effectiveness. When she loses her effectiveness, she becomes null and void.

CHAPTER 4

SPIRIT OF INTIMIDATION

One of Jezebel's most powerful weapons is the spirit of intimidation. This is where she overpowers her victims, and controls them. She will get them to the point where they will wear the makeup she thinks looks best, drive the car she thinks would be appropriate, wear the designer clothes she approves of, and become co-dependent on her.

The spirit of Jezebel is cunning, persuasive, smart, vindictive, and abusive. Every church has to pay attention to this spirit. Jezebel will work her way up through the ranks. She gets into the heart of the leadership, and gets into the hearts of the people. The whole time she has concocted a plan. Her eyes are like an eagle's, searching the congregation for prey. She is taking mental notes, as she scans. This woman will shake hands, hug people, kiss babies, lend an ear, give a little advice, and will always make herself available to people. You hear statements like "My door is always open to you," "Call me anytime," "You can trust me," "I won't tell a soul," and the most popular statement "I am here for you." Those people that are weak and rebellious will constantly confide in her. It appears to them Jezebel is like a girlfriend, a spiritual mother, a counselor, a confidant, a godsend, and everything you need in a leader.

She gives you personalization, and you have direct access to her. You begin to share very deep personal things with her. You share things that have taken place in your past, and in your present. You tell Jezebel about your children, your husband, your wife, your financial status, and anything that you would normally open up to tell your pastor. But because Jezebel is there in leadership, working with your pastor, you feel if I cannot get to pastor I might as well open up to her. Meanwhile Jezebel has added all this information to her data file, because she is setting you up for something that is going to overwhelm you.

After Jezebel has gotten enough people whom she can influence, she begins to do private outings, such as Bible studies, dinners at home, shopping trips, visits to different ministries, and a plethora of other activities. She will pray for the pastor, and pray for the church. Then she will have you praying against the pastor, and against the church. Then she will have her new recruits go recruit other people within the church. It is their job to recruit other people to come to the Bible studies. Jezebel is starting a church within a church.

When she is called on the carpet about it, she vehemently denies that she is starting a church. After being rebuked, she then goes to plan B.

Her plan is to orchestrate a church revolt. She then gets her selective group together, and reveals her plan to start her own church. Immediately they begin to shout in exuberance that they are behind her, and will support her in her endeavors. This group consists of rebellious women, codependent individuals, and Ahabs. These are men who are led around by their noses by their wives. They are not even real men, their wives make the decisions, control the money, and run the houses. He cannot even make a decision whether he should take the family to dinner or a movie. He has no sense of how to become a man. He grew up in a household where the grandmother controlled the grandfather, where the mother controlled the father. So he feels it is okay to bring his check home and his wife gives him forty dollars for the week. The man's self-esteem has been destroyed. His wife emasculates him every chance she gets. She emasculates him in front of his children, his friends, his family, and in the presence of Jezebel. What she is saying to the other women is that, I have control over my situation, and Jezebel approves of it.

Every woman wants a man that will lead her. One of the problems we have in society today is that no one wants to take the lead. After a man becomes a man, he understands that Ahab is an oxymoron, a contradiction in terms. When it comes to being a man, Ahab symbolizes weakness, and a man is symbolic of strength, leadership, and a warrior.

There are two definitions in Greek for the word man. The first is the word *anthropos* - which means man generically, regardless of his race, creed, or color. The second is the word *aner* - which means fully developed man. His hands cannot grow any longer, his feet cannot get any bigger. He is a fully developed man. Then the word *aner* goes another step, because it gives us the qualifications of a man. <u>The first qualification</u> is husband. Comes from the German word house-band, which means the man must band his house together. <u>The second qualification</u> is he must be a provider. A real man will do what he has to do to provide for his family. <u>The third qualification</u> for a man is he must be a warrior. He has to be willing to fight for what he believes.

After Jezebel starts her church, the converts begin to see another side of her, a side that was always there, but it was never brought to light. This woman deals with these individuals from a whole different angle. She uses the power of intimidation very well. She uses your own personal data file against you. Some of the most dark, intimate, deep secrets you have shared with her, Jezebel begins to use them to intimidate you.

She knows your weaknesses, she knows your faults, she knows your likes and dislikes because you have been nothing but a mere case-study. She has already done a psychoanalytical profile on you, your husband, and your children. She knows exactly how much time, effort, and money she can squeeze out of you.

This woman's goal is to take you for everything she can get. She begins to do several different types of intimidation. The first type of intimidation she does is <u>psychological</u>.

<u>Girl (30)</u>:

This young lady was a phenomenal singer. She had numerous offers to sing all over the world. She loved God, worshipped him with everything she had, and was perhaps one of the most anointed women of God. Her pastor constantly told her, "You are an anointed singer, but God does not want you to leave yet. You have a work to do here. Besides you are overweight, and God is not pleased with you. You are undisciplined in your eating. If God helps you lose the weight, then I will release you." The woman loses 135 pounds. The pastor begins to say to her, "Girl you look sick. If you start traveling people are going to talk about you." So she began eating again, and her weight kept fluctuating up and down. She finally said I am tired of this. She left the church and went out on her own, but because she was psychologically and emotionally intimidated by this Jezebel, she found herself back in that church.

This type of intimidation and abuse has several steps: It leads to distress, oppression, suppression, repression and depression.

The second type of intimidation is <u>pastoral intimidation</u>.

<u>Man (38)</u>:

A young man is anointed, appointed, and gifted in the things of God. He is a virgin, and has a powerful ministry. The pastor has allowed him to go out, to minister at a few churches throughout the country. Every time this young man goes out, the pastor receives a report of how powerful this young man's ministry is. The pastor hears about the souls that are being saved, the lives that were changed, and the people that were healed. She begins to make statements like you are getting puffed up, do not get big-headed because people are calling you.

As a matter of fact you will not be taking any outside engagements for the next three months. You no longer have the right to book your engagements.

Any appointments that you accept will come through my office. Jezebel spends the next few months looking over the numerous appointments. After the three-month period, she then allows him to go out again. This time he is forced to take an adjutant with him, one that the pastor selects. This adjutant's responsibility is to report the events of the services every night to her. The young minister finally grows weary of her deceitful tactics. When he decides that he will leave, she threatens him with the statement, "You can leave if you desire, I will be making calls all over the country, and inform pastors that you are moving in a spirit of rebellion." He therefore decides that he will stay with Jezebel's ministry.

Jezebel will never respect him, and will abuse and intimidate him even more, because he has to be made an example to every other leader in this church.

This is a classic case of pastoral intimidation. When God informs you that you must leave, you have to obey the voice of God. For every 20 doors that Jezebel closes, God will open 50 to you.

The third type of intimidation Jezebel uses is <u>physical intimidation</u>.

<u>Woman (28)</u>:

A weekly conference meeting is taking place. During the conference the secretary suggests that Jezebel pursue another option. In the presence of the staff, Jezebel immediately comes nose to nose with the secretary by saying, "This is my ministry, and I will run it the way I want to run it. I do not need you. I can replace you anytime I feel like it. If I need your opinion, I will ask you for it. This is the reason your husband left you in the first place. You run your mouth too much, and you are too opinionated. From now on in these meetings, you keep your mouth shut."

This is done in the presence of the staff, so that no one ever challenges her authority or gives their opinion. No one will ever confront her because no one wants to endure the wrath of Jezebel.

Fortunately this poor woman left the ministry, and did not look back. It took her several years to get healed from this spirit of intimidation. I am glad to report that she is one of the best business managers a church could ever have, and she has a husband that loves her, cherishes her, and adores the ground she walks on.

Out of the three cases we discussed, only one person was set free from the grasp of Jezebel. Do not succumb to the wiles of Jezebel, today is your day to be free. Jezebel brings about a spirit of confusion, pandemonium and frustration. It is time for you to walk in joy, peace and happiness.

And let the peace of God rule in your hearts, to which also you were called in one body; and be thankful (Colossians 3:15).

It is very important that you not allow yourself to be linked with anyone that is not pushing you toward the vision of the house. If the Bible study was not authorized by your pastor, do not go. If your pastor has not released them, do not partake in their schemes or wiles. Keep your eyes open for people that speak against leadership. Anyone that is not working for the good of the church, and working against it, is not only walking in a Jezebel spirit, but they are moving in the spirit of the Antichrist, and of the false prophet.

In my conclusion, if you have found yourself in the grasps of a Jezebelic spirit, it is time for you to be free physically, emotionally and financially.

Notes

Notes

ABOUT THE AUTHOR

Kervin J. Smith is the President of Kervin J. Smith Ministries, an international and inter-racial ministry that has become a prophetic voice being heard around the world. He travels extensively around the world, and is known for his keen and accurate prophetic insight and expository teaching.

A former financial consultant, who conducts financial seminars around the world. Kervin J. Smith has been given a strong mandate from the Lord to provide a clear prophetic voice to the Body of Christ.

Kervin Smith's nondemoninational approach has opened doors for his teachings to people from many different racial and religious backgrounds.

He has been invited to be a speaker in various venues, including churches, universities, and corporations. He has ministered to government officials, celebrities, professional athletes, and high level executives in Fortune 500 companies. Kervin has also been featured on many syndicated talkshows, radio forums, and symposiums, including the Trinity Broadcasting Network (TBN).

Kervin J. Smith is a prolific author, and has written several books such as *"Body Building: Getting the Church in Shape,* "Prophetic Power," and "Understanding the Three Types of Anointing."

OTHER BOOKS BY THE AUTHOR

Body Building : Getting the Church in Shape

Prophetic Power

Understanding the Three Types of Anointing

Autopsy of the 21st. Century Church
  (release date December 2003)